ANYBODY THERE?

FINDING MEANING IN A CONFUSING WORLD

DAVE MARTIN

A LION BOOK

Text copyright © 1995 Dave Martin
This edition copyright © 1995 Lion Publishing

The author asserts the moral right
to be identified as the author of this work

Published by
Lion Publishing plc
Sandy Lane West, Oxford, England
ISBN 0 7459 3319 X
Albatross Books Pty Ltd
PO Box 320, Sutherland, NSW 2232, Australia
ISBN 0 7324 1266 8

First edition 1995
10 9 8 7 6 5 4 3 2 1 0

All rights reserved

A catalogue record for this book is available
from the British Library

Printed and bound in Slovenia

Contents

1	Virtual Reality	5
2	Beam Me Up	10
3	Is Anybody There?	14
4	Fancy That	18
5	Megastar	22
6	Revealing	26
7	Rough Justice	30
8	Alive and Kicking	35
9	Solid Gold	39
	Reading the Bible: Getting Started	44

1 Virtual Reality

Want to walk on the moon, travel through your own body, or wrestle a bear? Ever wished you could design your own fourtrack and then drive it immediately over a rocky mountain range? Virtual Reality promises to make all this possible.

In fact, computer whizzos aim not just to make it the next best thing to being there, they say you won't be able to tell the difference. VR technology works directly on the senses to create the illusion of 'being there', so one day we might be able to do 'virtually' the things we cannot do in real life.

If VR turns out anything like today's

computer games, it will be totally addictive for some people. But the interesting thing is that, in the end, VR is only 'virtually' real. As in computer games, the computer will always do what you tell it. So, in most games, if you get blown away, chopped up or slimed at a certain stage, all you have to do is restart and try the same thing again and again until you get it right.

Best of all, of course, if you just can't get it right, or you get bored with losing, you switch off. Reality is not that predictable. In real life, crossing the road every day at the same time, in the same place, wearing the same clothes, whistling the same tune, will never produce the same results. It is impossible to recreate exactly the same conditions. Even the most brilliantly trained athlete cannot produce exactly the same results every time. The conditions are always changing and so is every aspect of the athlete's body.

Of course, life is not total chaos. There are certain things we can do and choices we can make that have a predictable outcome. We can eat to stop feeling hungry, we can put on clothes to keep warm, fire will burn and water will put it out. But what exactly tomorrow will bring, we don't know.

Reality is not always comfortable though. Illness, a sudden accident, friends falling out, or just simply waking up one morning in a bad mood – you cannot always tell what will happen next. It would be nice sometimes to be able to predict it, or to press the reset button, but we can't. We have to live with the boredom, put up with the pain, bury the things that hurt us and hope that the good times turn up more often than the bad.

Wouldn't it be good if there were something that helped make sense of reality and made it possible to face up to the knocks and pain? Wouldn't life really be worth living if you felt you were really loved so that whatever happened you could cope with life?

This book looks at some of the situations that we all find ourselves in and asks how life might be different. Believing in God is not just another game, but a way into reality.

Although life is unpredictable and some of us face tough situations, the love of God is guaranteed because he made us in the first place, and wants us to know him as a good father who loves his children.

When Jesus prayed to God, he called him Abba – Dad – and he told his followers to begin their prayers 'Our Father in Heaven'. He talked a lot about his Father and how much he loves us.

Your Father knows what you need before you ask him.

JESUS' WORDS IN MATTHEW'S GOSPEL

In the beginning God created the universe ... God created human beings, making them to be like himself ... God looked at everything he had made and he was very pleased.

THE BOOK OF GENESIS

2 Beam Me Up

The situation was getting tense. A couple in the carriage were having a fairly heated row and the conductor was having a hard time with two guys who were fare dodging. As the noise level grew, the smartly-dressed businessman in the opposite seat picked up his mobile phone, half smiled at me as he flipped it open and spoke into it: 'Beam me up, Scottie!'

Anyone who can afford it can own a mobile phone. Imagine you've just missed the last bus home and you don't know where the nearest phone box is to call for a lift, or a taxi.

Or there's been an accident; you need a phone. There's a great feeling of relief when you know someone can help you, or that blue or orange flashing light appears in the distance.

Being able to call on someone when things are getting difficult makes all the difference. Sometimes it's a bit hard to admit that the accident was your fault, or you have messed up, but knowing they are there helps. Sometimes you know that you are the only one who can get yourself out of the mess. You wish that you could be beamed up out of it, then you'd never have to see it again. But in real life most of us have to face our problems and difficulties and see them through.

When life gets tough, when you are afraid, anxious, or when you've messed up, there is someone who will help you. Just look at these words of Jesus: 'I will be with you always until the very end of time.' They were recorded in the Bible.

The whole story of the Bible is about how God wants people to live in permanent, close connection with him. They are not necessarily whisked out of their difficult situations and problems, although some amazing things do happen, but God is always available, ready to listen, to love and to help.

And Jesus is at the centre of the Bible story. The 'good news' of the Bible is that Jesus, born as a baby on earth, was God himself, and a human being. He knows what it's like to be human – the good bits and the bad bits. Mindblowing! The New Testament section of the Bible is all about Jesus. And it's through knowing Jesus that we can know God.

No one has ever seen God. The only Son [Jesus], who is the same as God and is at the Father's side, he has made him known.

FROM THE GOSPEL OF JOHN

He who has seen me has seen the Father.

WORDS OF JESUS

The Christmas story is so well known, we sometimes fail to notice how extraordinary it is – could the baby in the manger be the Son of God, the Saviour of the world? Read the story in Matthew's Gospel, starting at chapter 1, verse 18; and in Luke's Gospel, chapter 1, verse 26.

3 Is Anybody There?

Being ignored is bad news. There is nothing worse than being blanked out when you are trying to speak. There is nothing more discouraging than putting a lot of effort into a piece of work, or into how you look, and receiving no more than a glance or a grunt. Your parents are too busy, or just not around, or things just aren't talked about in your family. Sometimes you can survive on your own, especially if you have friends you can talk to. But we all need to be noticed.

Shaving your hair off, or having your eyebrow pierced, or stealing things, or bullying, or not eating, are ways to get noticed. Some of the things we do are because we want to be part of our gang of friends. Sometimes what someone else is wearing looks really neat, so we copy it. Other times, we just want to be ourselves and not always be told by some adult how we should look, or what we should do. Often we do things because we know we will be noticed and that, most of all, is what we want.

And we don't just want to be noticed. We want to be heard. Which means that somebody has to listen. Some of us need to talk more, most of us need to listen. All of us could cope with being listened to more. There was a poster campaign for a child care organization recently that had a picture of a teenage boy on it. The caption read: 'What he needs is a jolly good listening to.'

When Jesus Christ was on earth he was the expert at both talking and listening. He was interested in people. His stories, which seemed to be about everyday things but were really about God and about human nature, left people spellbound. People followed him around in massive crowds to hear what he had to say and his words of wisdom and his stories have lasted for thousands of years. Jesus had a way of seeing beyond all the things on the outside, so that people knew they could be themselves with him. And it's like that today. He is still with us; to listen, to help and show us the way.

Jesus told this simple story to show that we matter to God so much that he is always on the look out for us.

What do you think a man does who has a hundred sheep and one of them gets lost? He will leave the other ninety-nine grazing on the hillside and go and look for the lost sheep. When he finds it, he feels far happier over this one sheep than over the ninety-nine that did not get lost. In just the same way your Father in Heaven does not want any of these little ones to be lost.

4 *Fancy That*

I couldn't concentrate on my lessons for a whole term. I was totally put off. Verbs wouldn't conjugate, singular and plural were all the same to me. Studying French was both a nightmare and a great thrill. The French assistante was like a model and I was smashed. I landed on planet earth at the end of term when she left and was replaced by Mr Wainwright.

Most of us have a moment when we really fancy another person. Sometimes it turns into a serious relationship; most times it just fades into that place of many dreams. It wasn't a relationship based on reality.

Advertisements are designed to get us to fancy things too. The latest clothes, CD, computer game, perfume, even certain fizzy drinks. They all seem so attractive and we dream about how life would be if only we had them. Going out with a certain person, or wearing a particular pair of trainers, or owning the latest computer game can help us feel good, or keep us in with a group of friends.

Deep down, we know that there is more to life than that. Sometimes we don't care what other people think; other times a real friend who doesn't mind what we look like, or what we have, is more important than anything. Most of us have had a moment when we have felt really loved, or a time when we have felt really important, and usually it has been nothing to do with what we looked like, or what we owned.

But the world we live in tells us that if we want to be loved and valued we should spend our money on trying to look cool, owning the latest things and being seen with the right people.

If I think about it, when I was at school I liked my history teacher best. It was my worst subject and he knew it, but he had a great way of encouraging me. He always believed I was doing my best so I didn't mind being nearly bottom of the class, because he didn't make a big deal of it and show me up in front of everyone else.

There were no adverts in Jesus' day and I don't know if one pair of sandals was more fashionable than another, but Jesus talked a lot about how God accepts us for who we really are. People who came to Jesus with money and possessions soon discovered that he was more interested in the kind of person they were on the inside.

Jesus was interested in all sorts of people: rich, poor, good, bad, important, unimportant. He accepted and loved them all. Love is a word we throw around a lot, but most of us know that we want to be loved for the person we are on the inside and not for all the things we try to be.

People's true lives are not made up of the things they own, no matter how rich they may be.

WORDS OF JESUS, FROM LUKE'S GOSPEL

5 *Megastar*

A few years ago, Paul McCartney played to the largest paying audience ever for a live concert: 180,000 people in Rio de Janeiro, Brazil. Michael Jackson, whose album *Thriller* has sold over 47 million copies to date is said to be on a contract of over $800 million with Sony. He is followed by Madonna with her meagre $60 million contract with Time Warner.

It doesn't really matter whether it is music, or sport, fashion or films, every now and again another megastar appears. The megastar is the kind of person that everyone loves, or loves to hate; the kind of person who gives you a buzz or makes you tingle when they perform — you would do anything to be able to meet them or be with them.

You have the poster, wear the T-shirt, buy the fanzine and probably learn 101 useful facts about them. But sadly, as soon as the megastar is not at peak skill, or the fashion changes, we move on to the next person and they move into the record books.

We look to the megastars for all kinds of reasons — and they inspire us. If you are good at snooker, watching your hero helps you improve your game. If you are learning to play an instrument, your star encourages you to practise. Your favourite singer refuses to eat meat; you do the same.

The lifestyle of the rich and the famous attracts us. It may be just a dream, and in the end we know that life for a megastar has its ups and downs too, but the stars give us an injection of hope and happiness and we can imagine for a moment what life could be like – if only.

Of course, there are different sorts of megastars – different lifestyles, different messages. In his own lifetime, Jesus had a fairly large following for a travelling teacher and healer. What is amazing is that after such a short appearance in public – only three years – his following has grown and continued over nearly two thousand years.

Like the megastars today Jesus offered people hope, and a glimpse of what the world could be like. Unlike the megastars of our day, the song he sang didn't become dated.

Through Jesus, we can see that God cares about love, justice and peace. His message is revolutionary. It is about letting go of self-centredness, of being strong by being weak and depending on God, of having your sights set on doing things God's way. Someone has described this as 'the upside-down kingdom'. In Jesus' world, 'the first shall be last'. And, ultimately, Jesus put his message to the test by dying for his followers.

You are the salt of the earth... you are the light of the world... love your enemies and pray for those who persecute you... do not take revenge on someone who wrongs you. Do not store up treasures on earth... but store up riches in Heaven.'

WORDS OF JESUS, FROM MATTHEW'S GOSPEL

The greatest love a person can have for his friends is to give his life for them.

WORDS OF JESUS, FROM JOHN'S GOSPEL

6 *Revealing*

As soon as you are old enough to hold a bank account and your name appears on an accessible mailing list, the junk mail starts to arrive. The best deals around; ten CDs for the price of one; a free holiday; shares in an apartment in Portugal and, of course, you have been personally selected for the jackpot prize.

It is all very tempting, even if most of the time we know that nothing is really for free and that there is probably a catch somewhere. Sometimes, though, we take a chance in the hope that we might just get something, because inside us all there is the thought that we might be able to cut a corner to get some of the things we would really like.

What is really annoying and most tempting about the computerized letter is that it is often very difficult to tell just how personal it really is. Are you one of a handful, so that this letter is addressed directly to you and therefore you have a great chance of winning, or has the word processor simply merged your name into the text along with thousands of others?

You probably never will know, but one person does. The computer operator who put the whole thing together in the first place can tell simply by pressing a key. The screen fills with every instruction that the operator put into the computer. Not only is all the information revealed, but it is also possible to correct any mistakes and clear out any garbage that does not need to be there. What would happen if someone pressed the 'reveal' key on our lives? What would be displayed?

Most of us don't screw up on life in a big way. We've been told that it's the survival of the fittest so if we see an opportunity, we take it. Sometimes we make big mistakes, treat people really badly. Mostly it is just little things. Unless it's very serious and the law catches up with us, we try to forget about it. But somewhere, deep down, there's a feeling of guilt, a sense of failure. If only we could start again...

We can start again. We don't need to go on feeling guilty about things we've done in the past, so long as we are honest with God. He wants us to reveal ourselves to him, to admit the things we feel bad about. By coming clean, we will discover the fresh start that God is longing to offer us. But how can we know this for sure? Because God has revealed himself to us. This is where Jesus comes in. In the person of Jesus, God showed us his love.

Just as sure as Jesus always responded to people who called out to him for help when he was on earth, he will now help us and forgive us when we call to him and say we are sorry. His death on the cross proved once and for all that God was serious about dealing with the wrong in all of us. When he died he took it with him and since then any life can be cleared of the garbage that leads us to crash.

Forgive us our sins, as we forgive those who sin against us.

FROM THE LORD'S PRAYER

If anyone is in (believes in) Christ, he is a new creation; the old has gone, the new has come.

FROM PAUL'S SECOND LETTER TO THE CORINTHIANS

By Jesus' death we are put right with God.

FROM PAUL'S LETTER TO THE ROMANS

7 Rough Justice

Somewhere in the world a child dies every three seconds. In cocoa-producing countries like Ghana there are people earning only a few pence a day and living in desperate conditions so that we can drink our coffee and eat our chocolate. In Britain there are over 200,000 young people living and sleeping on the street. Two-thirds of them are teenagers. There's something wrong with the world.

Everybody knows. The TV and newspapers remind us every day what a terrible world we live in. The statistics are staggering, the faces freeze our feelings, the appeals appal and we feel helpless. But the signs are that we do care.

If people are prepared to go round wearing red plastic noses all day and cover themselves in baked beans, or push an old hospital bed for a hundred miles to raise money in response to these massive needs, they must be mad, but they must also care.

If whole communities will give over food and clothes, blankets, toys and equipment, and drivers will take days off work to take a huge lorry across miles of countryside filled with snipers just to give a bit of hope and comfort to people they've only ever seen on the TV, they may be foolish, but they must care.

The things that happen shouldn't happen – babies with no milk; children scared to death; disabled people left to rot; whole tribes of people massacred. Your list may be different, but you will be saying 'It's not fair' and you will probably be asking 'Why does it have to happen?' or 'Why does God allow it?'

Well, one thing is clear. Some of it doesn't have to happen. If we in the 'first world' were not so selfish and greedy and we could persuade our governments to talk the language of fairness and justice, then some of the starving would get food and some of the refugees would have homes and some of the hardest workers would get a decent wage and living conditions. It's up to us to do something about it.

But we are still left with some hard questions. Mystery diseases, years of no rain, freak accidents, surely a good God would stop these things happening?

The Bible tells us that when God made the world everything was perfect – there was no suffering. But then evil came into the world, and since then, in a mysterious way that no one really understands, things have gone wrong. Relationships between God and people, between people and people, and even in the world of nature, they have gone wrong.

When Jesus came into the world he

experienced everything as a human. He was treated unfairly too. Although he had done nothing wrong, he was put to death after he had been tortured and flogged, and then experienced the pain of being brutally nailed to a wooden cross. God the Son who knew excellent existence knew human pain and suffering on earth. And when he died, it looked as if evil had won.

But that wasn't the end. When Jesus rose from the dead three days later, he proved that injustice and suffering were not going to have the last word. What's more, he showed us that death isn't the end. He gave people hope.

When there are situations that seem beyond any help and beyond any logical explanation as to why they should be, we can guarantee that God will be there right in the middle of it all. He knows what it is to suffer. He feels the pain. Just as eventually the death of Jesus led to his resurrection, so God will also bring some purpose out of every situation of unfairness.

John, writing in the book of Revelation, looks forward to a future where God will bring everything back as he wants it:

Then I saw a new heaven and a new earth ... God will wipe away all tears from their eyes. There will be no more death, no more grief or crying or pain.

8 *Alive and Kicking*

Colours, images, faces. Cameras twisting, turning. Close up, pan back, spin round. Graphics, lasers, smoke machines.

Watching just one song on a music video can give you thousands of sights and sounds. The lyrics and the images tell a story, the music catches the mood, the beat gets you involved. The message of the song comes alive.

Dancing to the music, especially at a live concert, involves your whole self. The beat gets hold of you and you want to move, even if you know you're not very good at it. There is freedom just to enjoy doing your own thing and letting all your senses be turned on. You feel you're the only person in the whole world, or that you are one part of a massive body of beat, heat and sweat.

It's great to let go and have fun. It makes you realize that it's good to be alive. God has given us a brilliant world with things to excite all our senses. Technology can create colour, sound and sensation — almost anything is possible. All these things already exist in the world, in what we see, feel, touch and hear — winter's frozen water; spring's warm sun; the fruit and flowers of summer; the crazy colours of autumn. Out there is a world full of experience, creation and sensation that we haven't even started to get to grips with.

The sad thing is that some people feel the need to try and get even *more* out of the experience — a couple of 'E' to help you dance, a six-pack of lager to enjoy the match, or borrowing someone's GTI for a quick spin. Many people are looking for a kick from life, either because what they have experienced up to now has been pretty bad, or because nothing so far has helped them to feel life is that exciting.

And there are people who are out to exploit others and to make money out of them. These are the people who don't care who they harm. They make deadly drugs available and cheapen and abuse love and sex, which we were given to enjoy.

But being human and being alive is more than just the senses. There must be a point in living. A purpose in life. A reason for being. Where do we get a sense of identity? We have minds, bodies, souls. Being human, we've been created to find meaning in our existence.

When Jesus was put to death and then, three days later, God raised him back to life, it was not just a clever trick to impress the people of the time, but was proof of all the things that Jesus had been saying – that life is more than just a few kicks, or squeezing the most sensation from the moment, or having the right gear. It is about knowing that God's world has a purpose of love, forgiveness and justice for everyone.

Following Jesus is about knowing you are loved and valued as a person and that you fit into a world that has a plan and purpose. It's about knowing that this material life isn't all there is. There's a whole different dimension to life.

The new life that Jesus promises can bring fulfilment, purpose, meaning.

I have come in order that you might have life... life in all its fullness.

WORDS OF JESUS

9 *Solid Gold*

If you buy a new camera, or tape player or hair dryer, along with all the bits of paper and polystyrene that fall out of the box, you should find a guarantee. The maker promises that the equipment will not break down for a year, or longer if you are lucky. If you buy a gold ring, or chain, then you need a guarantee to prove that when it says it is gold that it is the real thing. A certificate or the hallmark will prove that it is solid gold.

The problem is, you cannot guarantee what's going to happen in life. Nobody can guarantee a life without pain and problems.

You cannot guarantee a relationship will be perfect, forever. People who fall in love, perhaps for the first time, will ask a friend how they are supposed to know if this is the real thing. Of course, no one can really say and that is one of the reasons why some couples discover that they cannot stay together for ever. Relationships take time, patience and lots of commitment.

If you have been through a relationship breaking up, you will know just how painful it is and will remember how much you wished that someone could have guaranteed that it was the real thing beforehand. And it is these experiences that make us cautious about risking anything else. After all, if you cannot guarantee things like friendship and love, is it going to be possible to guarantee that God won't let you down?

Well, all of life is a risk – that's what makes it more exciting than a predictable computer game. God didn't make us like robots, which means that we have choices to make. Even believing in God is a relationship that has to be worked at. To truly know him, we need to make a commitment to him. And the only way you can start is by believing and trusting and relying on what you know about God and his Son Jesus.

The nearest thing to an instruction manual is the Bible and that takes a lot of reading. Some of it is clear and you will feel like God is speaking directly to you. Other parts are more tricky and will need other people to help you to understand what it is about. If you've never really looked at the Bible, try reading Luke's Gospel.

Next to the Bible, talking to God in prayer and meeting with other Christians are the best ways to keep your relationship with God alive and kicking.

And the guarantee? Is there something that will prove that this is the real thing?

Jesus promised that once he was not physically around any more, we would still be aware of his presence, in the person of the Holy Spirit. It is that Spirit of Jesus working in us that is the hallmark guaranteeing all the things we have looked at already.

Relationships still have to be worked at. Difficulties are not just magicked away, we have to face them. The world does not suddenly become a place of peace and goodness, we must take action. But at the same time, we do have the guarantee that

God is with us.

By knowing Jesus and living life his way, you can tap in to that extra dimension. The world comes alive and has meaning and purpose. Because you know that you are loved for who you are and God is always ready to forgive you when you are sorry for going wrong, you are ready to risk a bit in playing your part in making the world a fair, just and happy place to live.

Life like that has got to be the most precious thing there is. With Jesus, that's guaranteed.

Whoever loves me will obey my teaching. My Father will love them, and I will come to them and live with them.

WORDS OF JESUS

Anyone who believes in Jesus will not be disappointed.

FROM PAUL'S LETTER TO THE ROMANS

Reading the Bible: Getting Started

• THE BIBLE IS A BIG BOOK

In fact, it's made up of lots of books, divided into the Old Testament and the New Testament. The best place to start is with the New Testament, with the Gospels.

Make sure your copy of the Bible is a modern translation – the Good News Bible or the New International Version.

• WHICH BOOK?

All Bibles have a contents page to help you find your way about. Look first in the New Testament section. Find Luke's Gospel. It's usually just called Luke.

• CHAPTER AND VERSE

All the books in the Bible have been divided up

into chapters and verses. This makes it easy to find your way about – when you've worked out how it's done. For example Luke 11:1 means Luke, chapter 11 and verse 1. If you find this in your Bible you'll see it's about Jesus teaching his disciples (or followers) to pray.

• WHERE SHALL I START?

One of the best places to start reading the Bible is with the Gospel of Luke. The word 'gospel' simply means 'good news'. There are four Gospels – Matthew, Mark, Luke and John. All of them tell the story of the life of Jesus – it's the same story, told from different angles.

• WHAT NEXT?

Then read another Gospel, or go on to Luke's next book – the Acts of the Apostles. The apostles were followers of Jesus who had been with him and seen all the wonderful things he had done during his life on earth.

Their 'acts' are the things they did after Jesus went back to heaven, sending the Holy Spirit to help them continue to spread the good news about Jesus. Without the events recorded in this book the Christian church would never have got off the ground. As it is, the good news of Jesus is still being passed on in country after country today.

- OTHER WAYS OF READING THE BIBLE

If you don't already do this, ask your church youth leader whether you can have a small group to read the Bible together. It helps to share your ideas, as well as your questions, with other people.

- WHAT DO YOU GET OUT OF IT?

Well, the Bible isn't just any old book. And it's not simply a list of 'do's and 'don't's. It's a way of getting to know Jesus and discovering God's way of living. So, as we read the Bible we can pray, asking God to speak to us, to show us about himself, to ask him how we should live.

Jesus said,

Anyone who comes to me and listens to my words and obeys them — I will show you what he is like. He is like a man who, in building his house, dug deep and laid the foundation on rock. The river overflowed and hit that house but could not shake it, because it was well built. But anyone who hears my words and does not obey them is like a man who built his house without laying a foundation; when the flood hit that house it fell at once — and what a terrible crash that was!